Excerpts from three of the stories:

From "The Warrior Within"

Sometimes life can be a punch in the face. I don't just mean the hard blows that we receive from life. I also mean actual punches that your mother lands on your chin. Trust me—life has thrown me a lot of punches, and so did my mom.

From "A Change of Attitude"

For my father, school was the worst kind of prison, so I was raised believing that school at its best was a drag. My dad thought that the purpose of graduating from high school was so you never had to go back to school again, and I adopted this working stiff's philosophy.

I followed my dad's example like a man who double-crossed the mob follows a cement block to the bottom of the river.

From "The Power Within"

Consider this basic truth about human nature: we all want to respect ourselves. We all want to live our lives in such a way that we think well of our behavior and others think well of us. We do not want to be disrespected or seen as bad people. An equally basic truth is that the only way we can get respect is to earn it.

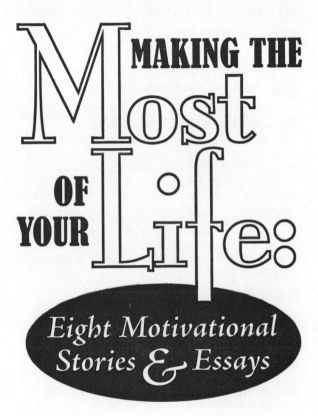

MAKING THE Most OF YOUR Life:

Eight Motivational Stories & Essays

Editor: John Langan
Afterword by Beth Johnson

 THE TOWNSEND LIBRARY

MAKING THE MOST OF YOUR LIFE:
Eight Motivational Stories & Essays

TP THE TOWNSEND LIBRARY

For more titles in the Townsend Library,
visit our website: **www.townsendpress.com**

"Dare To Think Big." Taken from *The Big Picture* by Dr.
Benjamin Carson; Gregg Lewis. Copyright © 1999 by
Benjamin Carson. Used by permission of The Zondervan
Corporation.

"Responsibility." Reprinted with the permission of Simon
and Schuster Adult Publishing Group from *The Road Less
Traveled* by M. Scott Peck, M.D. Copyright © 1978 by M.
Scott Peck, M.D.

Illustrations © 2008 by Hal Taylor

Townsend Press, Inc.
439 Kelley Drive
West Berlin, New Jersey 08091

ISBN-13: 978-1-59194-090-6
ISBN-10: 1-59194-090-7

Library of Congress Control Number:
2007930163

CONTENTS

ZERO

Preview

Bright and capable, the author of this essay followed the popular crowd— right into a career as a shopping-cart attendant at a giant warehouse store. There he ran into a glimpse of his past and had an unsettling vision of his future.

ZERO
Paul Logan

*T*hree *F's and two I's.*

My first semester grades hit me like a kick in the stomach. The *F's* were for classes where my work was poor. The *I's* were "incompletes" —for courses in which I never finished my assignments. They eventually became F's too.

I crumpled the report card and shoved it deep in a trash can. I can't say I was surprised. A zero grade point average was what I deserved, no question about it. But seeing my name in print on the worst possible report card still hurt. It also lit a spark in me, one that changed my life.

I was nineteen when I bombed out my first year of college. I hadn't always been a poor student. During elementary and middle school, I was consistently at the top of my class. But when I transferred into a huge regional high school, everything changed. I started "underachieving." Guidance counselors, teachers, and members of my family noticed. "You have potential," they'd say when they heard of my mediocre performance. "You just don't apply yourself."

They didn't understand. The truth was I *did* apply myself—just not to academics. As a shy, acne-prone teenager thrown into an enormous and unfamiliar high school, grades were not my priority; survival was. During my freshman year, I was constantly hassled and teased by a group of older guys at my school. They shoved and threatened me on the bus, teased me in the halls, and mocked me during lunchtime. *Nerd. Geek. Loser.* These insults were fired at me like bullets. Sometimes they came with fists. I got scared.

This fear transformed me. Constantly stressed and distracted, I stopped worrying about classes. Too embarrassed to admit to teachers or my family what was happening, I quietly dropped from an A student in 8th grade to C student just a year later. My definition of success changed just as dramatically. To me, a good day at school was no longer about doing well in class. It was simply about getting home without being hassled. To achieve this goal, I learned to blend in to the crowd—to look, talk, and act like the popular kids. First, I changed my clothes and hairstyle. Then I started behaving differently, hanging out with new "friends" and teasing the few kids who fit in worse than me. By the end of my freshman year, I escaped being at the bottom of the social ladder, but I also gave up on being a good student.

Instead, my focus was on following the crowd and being a social success. In 10th grade, I got a job at a nearby mall, so I could buy what seemed important: name-brand clothes, expensive sneakers, the latest CD's, and movie tickets—things I thought I needed to be popular. So what if my grades tumbled because I neglected my studies? At least no one was laughing at me anymore. By 11th grade, a new girlfriend and my used car were what I cared most about. Classes were a meaningless activity I endured weekdays. Senior year was more of the same, though I took the SAT and applied to a few colleges—because classmates were doing it. Despite my mediocre grades, I managed to get accepted. The following September, thanks to my family's savings, I followed the crowd and floated straight to college.

That's when I started to sink. Years of putting social time and my job ahead of school left me without study habits to deal with college work. Years of coasting in class left me unready for assignments that required effort and time management skills. Years of following others left me unequipped to make smart choices about my education. In addition to lacking skills, I also lacked motivation. College felt as meaningless to me as high school. Though I'd gotten accepted at a four-year university, nothing pushed me to succeed there. I arrived on campus in September without skills, goals, and a plan. I figured I could continue doing what I had done for years: coasting. It was a recipe for disaster.

My first week on campus, I coasted through freshman orientation, skipping activities because I didn't take them seriously. My second week, I attended a few parties, got home late, and overslept, missing a bunch of classes. No big deal, I thought. I'd just float by and hand in my homework late. But I quickly discovered, unlike high school, catching up was difficult in college. Readings in my English and History classes wore longer and more complicated than I was used to—too difficult for me to skim. Writing assignments were more numerous and required more time than I'd expected. Unaccustomed to the workload, I started cutting "easy" classes to complete overdue assignments from other courses. This strategy made me fall further behind, which, in turn, made it even more difficult to motivate myself to attend class.

Why bother if you're already behind? I thought.

Deadlines passed and work kept piling up, and I began to realize I was over my head. Halfway through the semester, I stopped going to classes regularly, hoping instead that I could score well on final exams to offset my missing assignments. But without attending class and taking notes, there was no way I could adequately prepare for tests. While coasting worked in high school, it didn't work in college. By the end of ten weeks, I knew I was done. No longer able to float, I'd sunk.

My family was stunned and disappointed at my failure. I was, too, though the lesson hadn't yet fully sunk in.

That happened a few months later when I was working at a large warehouse store called Sam's Club—the one place near home that would hire an unskilled college dropout in the middle of winter. My job was to retrieve shopping carts from the store's massive parking lot and stack them in rows for customers. Days and nights, I trudged across the dismal asphalt, collecting carts and cleaning up piles of garbage and soiled diapers shoppers left behind. On this March afternoon, it was raw and stormy, and I was wearing a used yellow Sam's Club raincoat that made me stink of sweat and vinyl. My hair was dripping, and my shoes squished like soaked sponges with each step.

The store was crowded with shoppers, and I'd just shoved a heavy train of carts next to the front door when a cluster of young people walked out. I recognized them immediately: four popular classmates who'd gone to my high school. They were giggling about something— a sound that brought me back to the time, years earlier, when I feared being laughed at by my peers. My face began to burn.

"Oh my God, it's *Paul*," said one of them. They all looked at me. I felt trapped.

"What are *you* doing here?" said Ken, a guy who'd been in my English class in 10th grade. He glanced at my rain-soaked jacket.

"Working," I said. There was an awkward silence. I had spent years trying to fit in with people like them, and now I only wanted to get away. "What about you?" I asked, hoping to change the subject.

"We're home for spring break," Ken replied.

The burning on my face suddenly grew hotter. They were already finishing their first year of college, and I was pushing carts in the rain—pushing carts for them.

"Paul, we need more carts in here! Hurry up!!!" my supervisor yelled from inside the store.

My former classmates looked uncomfortable and embarrassed. I could see the questions in their eyes. *What happened to you? Weren't you in college too?* I felt as if my first semester grade point average was written across my face and they were reading it.

Zero point zero.

I nodded a quick goodbye and turned away. My eyes stung as the truth of my mistakes poured down on me like the rain. I had allowed myself to become what my grade point average said: a failure—a dropout without a plan, a goal, or a real future. A zero. Coasting wasn't going to carry me any further. Neither would the CD's, the parties, or the brand name sneakers I'd so valued in high school. By pursuing them and nothing else, I'd closed doors in my life. If I kept following the same path, I could spend years struggling in that dreary parking lot or some other menial job while my peers moved forward. I wanted to do more with my life than push shopping carts.

The spark which ignited at the sight of my report card erupted into a burning flame in my chest. Watching my friends drive off that afternoon, one thing was suddenly clear to me: it was time to get serious and take control of my life. College could help me do that, I realized. It could be a lifeline; I just had to grab it—no more coasting.

The following fall, with money saved from working nine months in the parking lot, I paid for classes at a local community college. This time, I attended every orientation activity— and I took notes. Learning from past mistakes, I also bought a calendar and jotted down each assignment, so I could see deadlines well in advance and plan accordingly. Instead of skipping classes for social time, I arranged social events after class with peers who seemed serious about their work. No longer a follower, I became a study group leader! This actually helped me become a popular student—the thing I had chased for so long in high school.

I am not going to say it was easy. After long days on the job, I spent longer nights at home doing my coursework. It took months of practice for me to learn the skills I'd missed in high school: how to take good notes, how to take tests, how to write an effective essay, and how to get help when I needed it. But gradually I learned.

Throughout my second attempt at college, I sat beside many students who reminded me of myself during my first semester. I recognized them right away—students who seemed distracted or apathetic in class or who were frequently absent. They usually disappeared after a few weeks. Some were dealing with full lives that made it difficult to focus on their courses. Others, especially the ones straight out of high school, were coasting, unsure of why they were there or what they were doing. For these students, college is especially tough.

To thrive in college, you have to want to be there, and you have to be ready to focus on work. Some people aren't ready. They're likely to fail, just as I did. But even failure, as painful as it is, doesn't have to be an ending. It can be a learning experience—one that builds strength and gives direction. It can also serve as a wake-up call that turns a floating student into a serious one. It can even light a spark that sets the stage for future success. Take it from me, a former zero, who graduated from community college with a perfect 4.0 grade point average!

THE FIST, THE CLAY, AND THE ROCK

Preview

Often the best teachers are the ones who challenge us the most. In this selection, the author describes such a teacher. Mr. Gery inspires his students to work hard using nothing more than his fist, a lump of clay, a rock—and a few well-chosen words. Read how he does it.

THE FIST, THE CLAY, AND THE ROCK

Donald Holland

The best teacher I ever had was Mr. Gery, who taught 12th grade English. He started his class with us by placing on the front desk a large mound of clay and, next to it, a rock about the size of a tennis ball. That got our attention quickly, and the class quieted down and waited for him to talk.

Mr. Gery looked at us and smiled and said, "If there were a pill I could give you that would help you learn, and help you want to learn, I would pass it out right now. But there is no magic pill. Everything is up to you."

Then Mr. Gery held up his fist and kind of shook it at us. Some of us looked at each other. *What's going on?* we all thought. Mr. Gery continued: "I'd like you to imagine something for me. Imagine that my fist is the real world—not the sheltered world of this school but the real world. Imagine that my fist is everything that can happen to you out in the real world."

Then he reached down and pointed to the ball of clay and also the rock. He said, "Now imagine that you're either this lump of clay or you're the rock. Got that?" He smiled at us, and we waited to see what he was going to do.

He went on, "Let's say you're this ball of clay, and you're just sitting around minding your own business, and then out of nowhere here's what happens." He made a fist again and he smashed his fist into the ball of clay, which quickly turned into a half-flattened lump.

He looked at us, still smiling. "If the real world comes along and takes a swing at you, you're likely to get squashed. And you know what? The real world *will* come along and take a swing at you. You're going to take some heavy hits. Maybe you already have taken some heavy hits. Chances are that there are more down the road. So if you don't want to get squashed, you're better off if you're not a piece of clay.

"Now let's say you're the rock and the real world comes along and takes a swing at you. What will happen if I smash my fist into this rock?" The answer was obvious. Nothing would happen to the rock. It would take the blow and be unchanged.

He continued, "So what would you like to be, people, the clay or the rock? And what's my point? What am I trying to say to you?"

Someone raised their hand and said, "We should all be rocks. It's bad news to be clay." And some of us laughed, though a bit uneasily.

Mr. Gery went on. "OK, you all want to be rocks, don't you? Now my question is, 'How do you get to be a rock? How do you make yourself strong, like the rock, so that you won't be crushed and beaten up even if you take a lot of hits?'"

We didn't have an answer right away, and he went on, "You know I can't be a fairy god-mother. I can't pull out a wand and say, 'Thanks for wanting to be a rock. I hereby wave my wand and make you a rock.' That's not the way life works. The only way to become a rock is to go out and make yourself a rock.

"Imagine you're a fighter getting ready for a match. You go to the gym, and maybe when you start, you're flabby. Your whole body is flab, and it's soft like the clay. To make your body hard like a rock, you're got to train.

"Now if you want to train and become hard like the rock, I can help you. You need to develop skills, and you need to acquire knowledge. Skills will make you strong, and knowledge is power. It's my job to help you with language skills. I'll help you train to become a better reader. I'll help you train to be a better writer. But you know, I'm just a trainer. I can't make you be a fighter.

"All I can do is tell you that you need to make yourself a fighter. You need to become a rock. Because you don't want to be flabby when the real world comes along and takes a crack at you. Don't spend the semester just being Mr. Cool Man or Ms. Designer Jeans or Mr. or Ms. Sex Symbol of the class. Be some-one. *Be someone.*"

He then smashed that wad of clay one more time, and the thud of his fist broke the silence and then created more silence. He sure had our total attention.

"At the end of the semester, some of you are going to leave here, and you're still going to be clay. You're going to be the kind of person that life can smush around, and that's sad. But some of you, maybe a lot of you, are going to be rocks. I want you to be a rock. Go for it. And when this comes"—and he held up his fist—"you'll be ready."

And then Mr. Gery segued into talking about the course. But his demonstration stayed with most of us. And as the semester unfolded, he would call back his vivid images. When someone would not hand in a paper and make a lame excuse, he would say, "Whatever you say, Mr. Clay." Or "Whatever you say, Ms. Clay." Or if someone would forget a book, or not study for a test, or not do a reading assignment, he would say, "Of course, Mr. Clay." Sometimes we would get into it also and call out, "Hey, Clayman."

Mr. Gery worked us very hard, but he was not a mean person. We all knew he was a kind man who wanted us to become strong. It was obvious he wanted us to do well. By the end of the semester, he had to call very few of us Mr. or Ms. Clay.

THE WARRIOR WITHIN

Preview

For Dawn, being
abused was a way
of life. It took a
terrifying experience,
one that she barely
survived, to
convince her that
she could leave
the horrors of her
past behind.

THE WARRIOR WITHIN

Dawn Cogliser

Sometimes life can be a punch in the face. I don't just mean the hard blows that we receive from life. I also mean actual punches that your mother lands on your chin. Trust me—life has thrown me a lot of punches, and so did my mom.

I grew up in a really violent world. When I was one year old, my parents split up. To get a clean start with their lives, they decided to get rid of me. Luckily my grandparents stepped in and took me. I stayed with them until I was about six. Then good old Mom stepped back into the picture, deciding that she wanted to have a family again. The court granted her custody, and suddenly I was back with her. She got her wish of a family, including me and a new husband.

The dream family didn't work out so well for me. My stepfather was the most evil man I've ever met. Like Mom, he liked to throw punches. But his evil didn't end there. He decided to sexually molest me as well. So there I was, not yet eight years old, back with Mom and her new man, being beaten and molested. Nice family life, right?

I guess in that situation, some kids would have just shut down and become passive and withdrawn. But that was never my style, and that's probably something that helped save me. I was a fighter from the start. When my parents got rid of me, it made me tough. I had to be. To actually let myself feel the pain of what was happening would have been too much. So instead I grew tough and angry and took it out on anyone around me.

Although my mother had custody of me, the courts had given my grandparents weekends with me. So each weekend I was packed up and shipped off to their home. At the end of the weekend, I was shipped back to Mom's. And each time I arrived at the new home, I was grilled for at least a day about what went on in the other place. When my grandparents learned that I was being abused, they petitioned the court to give custody to them. The back-and-forth court battle went on longer than I can tell you. I remember being dragged into court over and over to tell the judge who I wanted to live with and why. And before each court date it was the same routine—my family members would drill me about what to say to make the others look bad. It was while all this was going on that I started to run away. Somebody would always find me and ship me back to my mother. Around this same time I discovered alcohol, and soon after that, drugs. Drugs and alcohol never solved my problems, but they helped me briefly escape the pain I was in. And escaping the pain was the only real motivation in life I had.

As I got closer to my teens, a new issue came up: my grandfather. He was my grandmother's third husband, so he wasn't actually a blood relative, but he was the only grandfather I'd ever known on my father's side. It was he and my grandmother who had taken me in when my parents gave me up. Like my stepfather, he was an alcoholic. Also like my stepfather, he was a molester. My stepfather did far more to me sexually than my grandfather, but just the fact that my grandfather tried to go down that road made me insanely angry and violent. From that point on I would lash out at anyone for any reason. If you looked at me wrong, I'd punch you in the face. Even if you were bigger than me and could beat my ass, when we were done you'd know I'd been there!

By the time I was in my teens, I was living on the streets more than in any home. I became a warrior, one who was ready for battle at all times. My "family" was the rough kids I hung out with. They were what I lived for. We had each other's backs, and as twisted as it seems now, they helped me go on with life. In order to keep them as friends, I had to be at least as tough as they were. The sense of safety I had when I was around them motivated me, simply because I was afraid that if I didn't keep up with them, I would lose them. This made me fight harder, drink longer, and always be the last one standing at the end of the night. No one knew that I was a crushed, scared kid inside.

I stayed in school, even though I never attended the same one for more than a year. I bounced up and down the East Coast, from family to family and friend to friend. Each time I got settled somewhere, I got into a fight and got thrown out, or ran away before I could get thrown out. But I stayed in school. Other kids skip school to hang out at home, but not me. School was my escape from home. It was the only place I could simply hang with my friends, get some lunch, take a shower, and be at peace. Sounds whacked, but I was motivated to go to school to get away from things. My grades were horrible, and I didn't understand much of what I was being taught, but I went every day.

I actually graduated. The same night, I left town. I caught a bus and went to some friends who lived in the projects in another city. I lived in the shadows there, never on anybody's lease, just couch-surfing from place to place, sleeping all day and partying all night. The fact is that I didn't expect to live past the age of 21. I was drinking and using drugs more heavily than ever, and fighting to the point that I was causing real damage to people. Secretly, I wished that someone would kill me during a fight. I was in that much pain from life. But I didn't show that pain. I couldn't. And the truth of it all is that there was something way down in my core that wanted to keep alive. Maybe, somehow, my inner warrior knew there was a worthwhile life out there for me.

I had just turned 19 when I met a guy at a party. I thought I was in love, and soon we were living together. For the first few years, everything was fine. We bought a house—the first house I'd ever lived in that no one could kick me out of. I felt like I had arrived. I had someone to share my life with, and a shot at a family of my own. We partied together.

Then his mother died, and something inside him snapped. He turned violent. His yelling at me and putting me down turned into pushing me and then punching me. My warrior, which had dozed off at that point, woke up with a vengeance. For the next four years we battled nonstop.

My friends couldn't understand why someone with my history of abuse would stay with a jerk who was beating the crap out of me. At first, I stayed with him because I thought I loved him. I believed the lies he fed me about how sorry he was he'd hit me and how he would never do it again. Furthermore, I thought it was normal for a man to beat his woman. That was all I had ever experienced. But there was a deeper reason I stayed. I battled that man because this was MY HOUSE, and I swore when I moved in that no one would ever take it away from me. I hated the fighting, but that wasn't anything new to me. In my mind I was warrior woman, and this man would not win. But at the end of it all, we had the mother of all battles. When it was over I was left lying in the woods, bloody and beaten and left for dead. But I did not die.

When I woke up in those woods, I realized that things had to change. I climbed into my car and drove away and never looked back. I had no idea where I was going; I just drove. And as I drove, I cried. I cried the kind of hard, sobbing tears that made my whole body shake. I tasted the blood and tears streaming into my mouth, and it was like tasting my life leaking away. That taste shocked me. I realized I had been willing to lose my precious life for a house. That feeling I had way down in my core, the one that wanted me to stay alive, was strong now. It told me that it was time to move forward. It was time to see what else life had to offer. It told me life wasn't about getting high or drunk or getting my ass beat or keeping someone else from winning. I knew there was something else, something for me, and I wanted to find it. I have never let myself forget the taste of that blood and those tears. The memory motivates me to keep moving forward towards all the great things that life has to offer me.

With the help of friends, I moved to a new area and began a new life. Another friend took me to visit his college campus, and I was blown away by the experience. I had never known anything about college, never given it a thought, but from that first moment I realized this was something I wanted. There was a sense of importance in the air, and I liked it. These people were doing something; they were working on their futures. I had never thought about my future, because I didn't believe I would have one. It would be years before I found the courage to start college myself, but just that glimpse inspired me.

I took a job in the corporate world that allowed me chances for advancement. Before I knew it, I was the assistant vice president of a high-powered firm. I got married and found myself living in a real home—not just a house, but a home filled with love. At age 35 I had my first child. I left my job to stay home and care for him. This was my dream life—I had a home, a great husband, and now I was a stay-at-home mom.

Still, this wonderful new life had its issues. For instance, when I was the vice president of a company, people treated me a certain way.

And now, even though mommies are the hardest-working people in the world, people treated me differently. I didn't know how to deal with this change in my identity. The great thing was that instead of turning to my old friends alcohol or drugs, I chose a new direction. I decided to take a college class. It was a basic English class, and the instructor was a young guy who had just started teaching. He seemed pretty cool, so I told him I didn't have any real education and might need some extra help along the way. And I did have problems—lots of them—and he did help me. I passed the class with a decent grade and really enjoyed the experience. It helped me realize that not only was I motivated, but that I was SMART!

Feeling encouraged, I took a few more college classes, and then met with a school counselor to see if there was a field I wanted to get a degree in. The idea of being a nurse really appealed to me, but I just knew there was no way I could do that. I obviously wasn't smart enough, or at least that's what I thought, and I was horrible at math.

But I really wanted to be a nurse.

So I waited until I had two choices: Drop out of college, or tackle the fundamental math class I was required to pass.

I took the class. I took it three times. But I finally passed it. And my inner warrior said, "It's time to take on nursing school." I applied to two schools and was accepted at both. Me—the "stupid" chick who partied and fought all the time. The schools could see my worth, even if I sometimes struggled to do that.

As I write this, I have just completed my first semester in nursing school with all B's and one A, and I am looking forward to next semester. Succeeding here has not only taught me about school stuff: it has taught me about myself. What I have learned is that despite all the mess and mistakes in my past, I matter in this world. I plan on making a big difference before I am done. My inner warrior is still fighting big time—but now it is for my future, not against my past. I have learned that I am not about what I came from. I am about where I am going.

DARE TO THINK BIG
Preview
This reading is by
Dr. Ben Carson, who
grew up poor with his
single mother in inner-
city Detroit. He was
considered the
"dummy" of his fifth-
grade class until he
realized he could learn
and do well in school.
Today, he is one of the
world's most respected
surgeons. In this
excerpt from his book
The Big Picture,
he shares a message
with students of today.

DARE TO THINK BIG

Dr. Ben Carson

I do not speak only to parent groups. I spend a lot of time with students, such as those I encountered not long ago on a memorable visit to Wendell Phillips High School, an inner-city school on Chicago's south side.

Before I spoke, the people who invited me to the Windy City held a reception in my honor. There I met and talked with school officials and local religious leaders, many of whom informed me about the troubled neighborhood where the school is located. They indicated that gang influence was prevalent, living conditions were deplorable in the surrounding public housing developments, dropout statistics were high, and SAT scores were low.

It sounded like a lot of other high schools I have visited around the country. Yet so dire were these warnings that, on the crosstown drive to the school, I could not help wondering what kind of reception I would receive from the students.

I need not have worried. When I walked into Wendell Phillips High School, its long, deserted hallways gave the building a cavernous, empty feel. The entire student body (1,500 to 2,000 strong) had already been excused from class and was assembled quietly in the school's auditorium. A school administrator, who was addressing the audience, noted my entrance through a back door and abruptly interrupted his remarks to announce, "And here's Dr. Carson now!"

All eyes turned my way. Immediately students began to applaud. Some stood. Suddenly they were all standing, clapping, and cheering. The applause continued the entire time I walked down the aisle and climbed the steps onto the auditorium stage. I couldn't remember ever receiving a warmer, more enthusiastic, or more spontaneous reception anywhere in my entire life.

I found out later that a local bank had purchased and distributed paperback copies of my autobiography, *Gifted Hands*, to every student at Wendell Phillips. A lot of those teenagers had evidently read the book and felt they already knew me. By the time I reached the microphone, the noise faded away. I felt overwhelmed by their welcome.

I did what I often do when facing such a young audience. I wanted them thinking seriously about their lives and futures. So I quickly summarized my earliest years as a child, about my own student days back at Southwestern High School in Detroit. I referred briefly to the incident when my anger nearly caused a tragedy that would have altered my life forever. I recounted my struggles with peer pressure, which sidetracked me for a time.

Then I talked about the difference between being viewed as cool and being classified as a lowly nerd. I find that serves as a graphically relevant illustration for my message on delayed gratification—a theme I hit almost every time I speak to young people.

The cool guys in every school are the ones who have earned a varsity letter in some sport—maybe several sports. They wear the latest fashions. They know all the hit tunes. They can converse about the latest block-buster movies. They drive sharp cars and seem to collect a bevy of beautiful girlfriends.

The nerds are the guys always hauling around an armload of books, with more in their backpacks. They wear clean clothes—and often big, thick glasses. They even under-stand the science experiments. They ride the school bus, or worse yet, their parents drive them to school. Most of the popular girls would not be caught dead speaking to them in the hallway between classes.

The years go by, and graduation draws near. Often the cool guy has not done well in school, but his personality wins him a job at the local fast-food franchise, flipping ham-burgers and waiting on customers. The nerd, who has won a scholarship, goes off to college.

A few more years go by. The cool guy is still flipping burgers. Maybe he has even moved up to Assistant Shift Manager by now. The girls who come in to eat lunch may notice and smile at him. He is still cool.

The nerd finishes up at college and does very well. Upon graduation he accepts a job offer from a Fortune 500 company. With his first paycheck, he goes to the eye doctor, who replaces those big, old, thick glasses with a pair of contacts. He stops at the tailor and picks out a couple of nice suits to wear. After saving a big chunk of his first few paychecks, he makes a down payment on a new Lexus. When he drives home to visit his parents, all the young women in the old neighborhood say, "Hey, don't I know you?" Suddenly, they do not want to talk to the guy behind the fast-food counter anymore.

The first guy—the cool guy—had everything back in high school. So what did he get for all that?

The other guy was not cool at all—but he was focused. Where did he go in the long run?

"And that," I told my audience, "is how we have to learn to think about life! With a long-term view. A Big-Picture perspective!"

Those students at Chicago's Wendell Phillips High School could not have been more attentive as I recounted the things this former nerd has seen and done. They listened to me explain and illustrate the incredible potential that resides in the average human brain. They even seemed receptive to my challenge that they begin to use those brains to plan and prepare for the future. So, as I wrapped up my talk by daring them to THINK BIG, I did something I had never done before, though I realized it could backfire if I had read this audience wrong. But since they had been such a responsive group, I decided to risk it.

I concluded by asking that auditorium full of high school students for a show of hands. "How many of you are ready, here today, to raise your hands and say to me, to your teachers, and to your peers, 'I want to be a nerd'?"

Although many of them laughed, almost all the students of Wendell Phillips High School raised their hands as they stood and applauded and cheered even louder than when I had walked in.

RAISING THE BLINDS

Preview

The beginning of college is an exciting time. But for many students it's also a challenging and difficult period. Author Peggy Kern describes her search for love and security during her freshman year—a search that led her to a painful decision.

RAISING THE BLINDS

Peggy Kern

I will never forget my first day at college. I was 18 years old, and my mother had driven me four hours to the small liberal arts school on the outskirts of Philadelphia where I would spend the next four years. The campus was beautiful: large stone buildings lined a lush, grassy square; huge trees blossomed along pathways to modern-looking dormitories. Everywhere, students gathered in small groups or lounged on blankets, laughing, reading, chatting. Proud parents unloaded supplies from the backs of station wagons— pillows, blankets, microwave ovens, posters— and waved to their kids as they finally, reluctantly, pulled away from the curb. This was college, and I was excited to be here.

The past year had not been easy at home. After many years of quiet distaste for one another, my parents had decided to separate after 20 years of marriage. They hadn't been close for a long time, but things had gotten worse during my senior year of high school. They argued a lot, at first quietly, in the bedroom with the door closed. But the fights became more intense; Mom would scream and yell and storm into the hallway, slamming the door behind her. Dad never yelled back; he stayed silent, as if there was no point in trying to fix it anymore.

My brother and sister were already away at college, so I was alone in the house as my parents' marriage exploded. Mom would spend long nights crying in her room; Dad moved into the basement and no longer ate dinner with us. Sometimes, he wouldn't come home at all. They both hired lawyers. The legal bills started to mount, and money became a constant concern. Eventually, Dad moved out and started dating a woman he worked with, which put Mom over the edge. My mother was filled with anger and sadness; I, too, felt betrayed by my father and confused by what was happening around me. I did not know what to do, or how to help, so I did the only thing I could think of: I made myself as small and unnoticeable as possible. If I don't do anything wrong, I thought, maybe they'll at least keep loving *me*.

I had become the invisible girl in my family. I kept on smiling and tried to stay out of the way. I spent a lot of time in my room, sometimes listening for long hours as she vented about my father on the phone. It was overwhelming and scary to watch my parents' marriage fall apart. I wanted to fix it, I wanted my mom to stop crying, I wanted my dad to come home. But most of all, I wanted someone to talk to. I felt empty and confused, lost and forgotten in the storm of my parents' divorce.

College felt like freedom from all of this, and for the first few weeks, I blossomed in my new environment. I spent hours decorating my dorm room. I had a different-colored notebook for each class. I had a tower of thick textbooks with intriguing names like *The Poetry of War*. I even made a few friends, and together we would talk about literature, philosophy, and which professors we would take again next year. For the first time in my life, I felt like an adult; I was on my own, finally in charge of my destiny, away from the chaos of home. But still, a part of me was sad. I missed my old friends from high school. I even missed my parents. But most of all, I missed feeling important, really *important*, to someone.

It had been a lonely year for me.

Then I met Tommy, a tall, handsome boy in my American History class. Tommy and I connected instantly. He was extremely smart and witty, and he seemed to hang on every word I said, as if I was genuinely interesting. But there was also something very sad about Tommy, a loneliness that I strongly identified with, as if he too knew what it felt like to be invisible. It didn't take long for us to begin dating, and soon, Tommy and I were together all the time. We couldn't get enough of each other. We would spend hours together, talking about our families and secret worries, or saying nothing at all. We would also talk about the future. Tommy wanted to become a history teacher; I planned to be a writer. We would help each other study and graduate from college together. Maybe someday we would get married and have a family. Tommy was a dream come true for me: he seemed to understand me as no one else ever had. He *needed* me, he said. And that made me feel wonderful.

At first, Tommy and I would go to parties together and hang out with friends. But soon we were spending most of our time sequestered in his dorm room with the shades drawn. Tommy didn't like to socialize much. *All I want is you*, he would say whenever I suggested a night out. Gradually, almost without my even noticing, I stopped hanging out with my friends and began to skip classes so I could spend more time with him. We slept all day and neglected our coursework. We ate every meal together. I worried about my grades suffering, but nothing else felt as good as being with Tommy. So what if I skipped class today? I'd just make up the work later on. If I failed, well, there was always next semester. Cocooned in Tommy's dorm room, it was easy to forget about student loans or grade point averages. All that mattered was right now, this moment. And besides, didn't I deserve this type of love and attention?

When my grades finally arrived over Christmas break, I was stunned: I had failed three of my five classes. I would have to take them over—and pay for them again as well. I was embarrassed and angry at myself. My mom had been so proud of me when I was accepted into college. *This is your time to shine, baby,* she had said. *I know the divorce has been hard on you.* She had spent so much time applying for student loans and financial aid so I could have the chance to attend a university. Even in the midst of the divorce, Mom had been adamant about my going to school. Now I had wasted my entire first semester.

I questioned my relationship with Tommy. He didn't seem to care at all if he flunked out of school. He would even get annoyed if I suggested that we study more or spend a few evenings apart. *Maybe we should just break up if you're that unhappy,* he would say, his voice a mixture of sadness and pride. I loved Tommy. I did not want to break up with him. But I did not want to flunk out of college either.

I managed to hide my dismal first-semester grades from my mother. She simply took my word for it that I was doing well, and she beamed with pride as a result. *I told you you'd love college,* she proclaimed, and I quickly smiled and nodded my head in agreement. I didn't want to worry her. But deep down, I wished that she would see that I was struggling. I wanted her to rescue me. But how could I admit that I had failed my classes? How could I admit that I was spending all my time with my boyfriend?

I swore to myself that I would do better next semester, but nothing changed at all. Tommy and I fell back into our old routine: skipping class, hiding out, lost in our own little world. My friends had officially given up on me, which meant that Tommy was now my only companion. I was hopelessly behind on my schoolwork. I tried to catch up, but this made Tommy insecure. If I spent an afternoon alone in the library, Tommy would be cold towards me, as if I was choosing schoolwork over him. I wanted him to believe that I loved him, but it seemed like the only way I could convince him of that was by giving him all of my time and energy. *I just want to be with you. Is that so bad?*, he would say, his voice sounding hurt if I argued.

Sometimes, it takes an earthquake to wake a person up. My earthquake came in the spring of my freshman year. I was standing in Tommy's dorm room, the shades drawn as usual, when the past year finally came crashing down around me. I was pregnant.

And absolutely terrified.

Tommy was shocked too, but he also seemed oddly relieved, as if the pregnancy was a solution, not a problem. *We could get married,* Tommy suggested, sounding more upbeat than he usually did. I was sobbing hysterically. *Maybe your mom could help us out while I find a job. We'll buy a little house somewhere eventually. Maybe this was supposed to happen, so we can be together forever.* Tommy sincerely believed what he was saying. I buried my head in his arms and closed my eyes tightly: if only I could stay in this room forever, where there were no consequences or complexity, only fantastic promises and the comfort of being in love. It had been enough for me for the past year, but not anymore. I was 18 years old, and I was pregnant. I was in serious trouble, and I could not wish it away.

I loved Tommy, but I also understood—finally, tragically, and a bit too late—that for the past year, I had pretended that everything was okay when in reality, my life was out of control. I did not blame him for the choices I had made. He did not force me to skip class. *I* chose to neglect my schoolwork and give up my friends. However, I also understood that Tommy loved me best when I was helpless and isolated. Tommy was depressed, and he wanted me to sit in the dark with him.

It was time for me to put myself first. I needed to choose my own future. I was tired of keeping the blinds drawn. I was sick of feeling small and unsure. I was tired of feeling like I had to choose between my own success, and Tommy's approval. I wanted to be in college. I wanted to achieve my dream of being a writer someday. I wanted to make my parents proud.

And I did not want to have a baby.

At that moment, I knew that I would have an abortion. The decision was difficult and frightening, and it stays with me to this day. It may, indeed, be with me forever. Tommy was not happy when I told him my intentions, but he supported me as best he could. I also decided to move back home for a while, and tell my mother the truth about my grades. I felt like a failure, but I also felt tremendous relief. No more hiding, no more depression. I had to take hold of my life. It was time to break up with Tommy, and make a real commitment to myself.

When I look back at my first year of college, I have mixed emotions. I wish I could have stayed in Philadelphia and graduated with my friends. I wish that I had never gotten pregnant. But I am grateful for the lessons I learned during my freshman year. After I moved back home, I took a part-time job and began attending a local community college. I committed myself to my studies, and eventually I earned a scholarship to a four-year university. I went on to earn a bachelor's degree in English. But most importantly, I enjoyed every single day of my college career. Each class felt like a gift; each exam, a privilege to take. I had come so close to missing this opportunity. I savored each day as a result.

I do not blame my parents for the mistakes I have made. I don't blame Tommy either. Ultimately, I am the one who must steer my own life. The choices I make have very real consequences, not just for today, but for years to come. Cocooned in Tommy's dorm room with the blinds closed, I had managed to forget that for a while.

It is a lesson I will not forget again.

RESPONSIBILITY

Preview

The Road Less Traveled,
a well-known book by
psychiatrist and author
M. Scott Peck, begins
with this famous line:
"Life is difficult." Peck
encourages people to
embrace the messy
difficulties that make
up life, stressing that
growth and development
are achieved only
through hard work. The
following excerpt from
The Road Less Traveled
emphasizes one of Peck's
favorite themes: personal
responsibility.

RESPONSIBILITY
M. Scott Peck

We cannot solve life's problems except by solving them. This statement may seem idiotically self-evident, yet it is seemingly beyond the comprehension of much of the human race. This is because we must accept responsibility for a problem before we can solve it. We cannot solve a problem by saying, "It's not my problem." We cannot solve a problem by hoping that someone else will solve it for us. I can solve a problem only when I say, "This is my problem and it's up to me to solve it." But many, so many, seek to avoid the pain of their problems by saying to themselves: "This problem was caused by other people, or by social circumstances beyond my control, and therefore it is up to other people or society to solve this problem for me. It is not really my personal problem."

The extent to which people will go psychologically to avoid assuming responsibility for personal problems, while always sad, is sometimes almost ludicrous. A career sergeant in the army, stationed in Okinawa and in serious trouble because of his excessive drinking, was referred for psychiatric evaluation and, if possible, assistance. He denied that he was an alcoholic, or even that his use of alcohol was a personal problem, saying, "There's nothing else to do in the evenings in Okinawa except drink."

"Do you like to read?" I asked.

"Oh yes, I like to read, sure."

"Then why don't you read in the evening instead of drinking?"

"It's too noisy to read in the barracks."

"Well, then, why don't you go to the library?"

"The library is too far away."

"Is the library farther away than the bar you go to?"

"Well, I'm not much of a reader. That's not where my interests lie."

"Do you like to fish?" I then inquired.

"Sure, I love to fish."

"Why not go fishing instead of drinking?"

"Because I have to work all day long."

"Can't you go fishing at night?"

"No, there isn't any night fishing in Okinawa."

"But there is," I said. "I know several organizations that fish at night here. Would you like me to put you in touch with them?"

"Well, I really don't like to fish."

"What I hear you saying," I clarified, "is that there are other things to do in Okinawa except drink, but the thing you like to do most in Okinawa is drink."

"Yeah, I guess so."

"But your drinking is getting you in trouble, so you're faced with a real problem, aren't you?"

"This damn island would drive anyone to drink."

I kept trying for a while, but the sergeant was not the least bit interested in seeing his drinking as a personal problem which he could solve either with or without help, and I regretfully told his commander that he was not amenable to assistance. His drinking continued, and he was separated from the service in mid-career.

A young wife, also in Okinawa, cut her wrist lightly with a razor blade and was brought to the emergency room, where I saw her. I asked her why she had done this to herself.

"To kill myself, of course."

"Why do you want to kill yourself?"

"Because I can't stand it on this dumb island. You have to send me back to the States. I'm going to kill myself if I have to stay here any longer."

"What is it about living on Okinawa that's so painful for you?" I asked.

She began to cry in a whining sort of way. "I don't have any friends here, and I'm alone all the time."

"That's too bad. How come you haven't been able to make any friends?"

"Because I have to live in a stupid Okinawan housing area, and none of my neighbors speak English."

"Why don't you drive over to the American housing area or to the wives' club during the day so you can make some friends?"

"Because my husband has to drive the car to work."

"Can't you drive him to work, since you're alone and bored all day?" I asked.

"No. It's a stick-shift car, and I don't know how to drive a stick-shift car, only an automatic."

"Why don't you learn how to drive a stick-shift car?"

She glared at me. "On these roads? You must be crazy."

A CHANGE OF ATTITUDE

Preview

No one was more surprised than Grant Berry to find himself in college. His high school experience did little to prepare him for a life of learning. But somehow, as father of two with a full-time job, he returned to school to pursue a college degree. Berry's transformation from a reluctant student to a passionate one is the subject of this essay.

A CHANGE OF ATTITUDE

Grant Berry

For me to be in college is highly improbable. That I am doing well in school teeters on the illogical. Considering my upbringing, past educational performance, and current responsibilities, one might say, "This guy hasn't got a chance." If I were a racehorse and college was the track, there would be few who would pick me to win, place, or show.

When I told my dad that I was going back to school, the only encouragement he offered was this: "Send me anywhere, but don't send me back to school." For my father, school was the worst kind of prison, so I was raised believing that school at its best was a drag. My dad thought that the purpose of graduating from high school was so you never had to go back to school again, and I adopted this working stiff's philosophy.

I followed my dad's example like a man who double-crossed the mob follows a cement block to the bottom of the river. My dad has been a union factory worker for more than two decades, and he has never striven to be anything more than average. Nonetheless, he is a good man; I love him very much, and I respect him for being a responsible husband and father. He seldom, if ever, missed a day of work; he never left his paycheck at a bar, and none of our household appliances were ever carted off by a repo-man. He took his family to church each week, didn't light up or lift a glass, and he has celebrated his silver anniversary with his first, and only, wife. However, if he ever had a dream of being more than just a shop rat, I never knew about it.

On the other hand, my dreams were big, but my thoughts were small. I was not raised to be a go-getter. I knew I wanted to go to work each day in a suit and tie; unfortunately, I could not define what it was I wanted to do.

I told a few people that I wanted to have a job where I could dress suavely and carry a briefcase, and they laughed in my face. They said, "You'll never be anything," and I believed them. Even now I am envious of an immaculately dressed businessman. It is not the angry type of jealousy; it is the "wish it were me" variety.

Since I knew I was not going to further my education, and I didn't know what I wanted to do except wear a suit, high school was a disaster. I do not know how my teachers can respect themselves after passing me. In every high school there are cliques and classifications. I worked just hard enough to stay above the bottom, but I did not want to work hard enough to get into the clique with the honor roll students.

Also, I had always had a problem with reading. When I was a kid, reading for me was slow and tedious. My eyes walked over words like a snail trudging through mud. I couldn't focus on what I was reading, which allowed my young, active mind to wander far from my reading material. I would often finish a page and not remember a single word I had just read. Not only was reading a slow process, but my comprehension was nil. I wasn't dumb; in fact, I was at a high English level. However, reading rated next to scraping dog poop from the treads of my sneakers. I didn't yet know that reading could be like playing the guitar: the more you do it, the better you get. As far as reading was concerned, I thought I was stuck in the same slow waltz forever.

In junior high and high school, I read only when it was absolutely essential. For example, I had to find out who Spiderman was going to web, or how many children Superman was going to save each month. I also had to find out which girls were popular on the bathroom walls. I'm ashamed to say that my mother even did a book report for me, first reading the book. In high school, when I would choose my own classes, I took art and electronics rather than English.

Even though I was raised in a good Christian home, the only things I cared about were partying and girls. I spent all of my minimum-wage paycheck on beer, cigarettes, and young ladies. As a senior, I dated a girl who was 20. She had no restrictions, and I tried to keep pace with her lifestyle. I would stay out drinking until 3:00 a.m. on school nights. The next morning I would sleep through class or just not show up. It became such a problem that the school sent letters to my parents telling them that I would not be joining my classmates for commencement if I didn't show up for class once in a while. This put the fear of the establishment in me because I knew the importance of graduating from high school. Nonetheless, I never once remember doing homework my senior year. Yet in June, they shook my hand and forked over a diploma as I smugly marched across the stage in a blue gown and square hat.

Since I felt I didn't deserve the piece of paper with the principal's and superintendent's signatures on it, I passed up not only a graduation party, but also a class ring and yearbook. If it were not for my diploma and senior pictures, there would not be enough evidence to convince a jury that I am guilty of attending high school at all. I did, however, celebrate with my friends on graduation night. I got loaded, misjudged a turn, flattened a stop sign, and got my car stuck. When I pushed my car with my girlfriend behind the steering wheel, mud from the spinning tire sprayed all over my nice clothes. It was quite a night, and looking back, it was quite a fitting closure for the end of high school.

After graduation I followed my father's example and went to work, plunging into the lukewarm waters of mediocrity. All I was doing on my job bagging groceries was trading dollars for hours. I worked just hard enough to keep from getting fired, and I was paid just enough to keep from quitting.

Considering the way my father felt about school, college was a subject that seldom came up at our dinner table. I was not discouraged, nor was I encouraged to go to college; it was my choice. My first attempt at college came when I was nineteen. I had always dreamed of being a disc jockey, so I enrolled in a broadcasting class. However, my experience in college was as forgettable as high school. My habit of not doing homework carried over, and the class was such a yawner that I often forgot to attend. Miraculously, I managed to pull a C, but my dream was weak and quickly died. I did not enroll for the next term. My girlfriend, the one who kept me out late in high school, became pregnant with my child. We were married two days after my final class, which gave me another excuse not to continue my education.

My first job, and every job since, has involved working with my hands and not my head. I enjoyed my work, but after the money ran out, the month would keep going. One evening my wife's cousin called and said he had a way that we could increase our income. I asked, "How soon can you get here?" He walked us through a six-step plan of selling and recruiting, and when he was finished, my wife and I wanted in. Fumbling around inside his large briefcase, he told us we needed the proper attitude first. Emerging with a small stack of books, he said, "Read these!" Then he flipped the books into my lap. I groaned at the thought of reading all those volumes. If this guy wanted me to develop a good attitude, giving me books was having the opposite effect. However, I wanted to make some extra cash, so I assured him I would try.

I started reading the books each night. They were self-help, positive-mental-attitude manuals. Reading those books opened up my world; they put me in touch with a me I didn't know existed. The books told me I had potential, possibly even greatness. I took their message in like an old Chevrolet being pumped full of premium no-lead gasoline. It felt so good I started reading more. Not only did I read at night, I read in the morning before I went to work. I read during my breaks and lunch hour, waiting for signal lights to turn green, in between bites of food at supper, and while sitting on the toilet. One of the books I read said that there is no limit to the amount of information our brains will hold, so I began filling mine up.

The process of reading was slow at first, just as it had been when I was a kid, but it was just like playing the guitar. If I struck an unclear chord, I would try it again, and if I read something unclear, I would simply read it again. Something happened: the more I read, the better I got at it. It wasn't long before I could focus in and understand without reading things twice. I began feeling good about my reading skills, and because of the types of books I was reading, I started feeling good about myself at the same time.

The income from my day job blossomed while the selling and recruiting business grew demanding, disappointing, and fruitless. We stopped working that soil and our business died, but I was hooked on reading. I now laid aside the self-help books and began reading whatever I wanted. I got my first library card, subscribed to *Sports Illustrated*. I found a book of short stories, and I dove into poetry, as well as countless newspaper articles, cereal boxes and oatmeal packages. Reading, which had been a problem for me, became a pleasure and then a passion.

Reading moved me. As I continued to read in a crowded lunchroom, sometimes I stumbled across an especially moving short story or magazine article. For example, a young Romanian girl was saved from starvation and deprivation by an adoptive couple from the U.S. I quickly jerked the reading material to my face to conceal tears when she entered her new home filled with toys and stuffed animals.

Not only did reading tug at my emotions; it inspired me to make a move. All those positive-mental-attitude books kept jabbing me in the ribs, so last fall, at age 27, I decided to give college another try. Now I am back in school, but it's a different road I travel than when I was a teenager. Mom and Dad paid the amount in the right-hand column of my tuition bill then, but now I am determined to pay for college myself, even though I must miss the sound of the pizza delivery man's tires on my blacktop driveway. I hope to work my way out of my blue collar by paying for school with blue-collar cash.

As a meat-cutter, I usually spend between 45 and 50 hours a week with a knife in my hand. Some weeks I have spent 72 hours beneath a butcher's cap. In one two-week period I spent 141 hours with a bloody apron on, but in that time I managed to show up for all of my classes and get all of my homework done (except being short a few bibliography cards for my research paper).

Working full time and raising a family leaves me little free time. If I'm not in class, I'm studying linking verbs or trying to figure out the difference between compound and complex sentences.

There are other obstacles and challenges staring me in the face. The tallest hurdle is a lack of time for meeting all my obligations. For instance, my wife works two nights a week, leaving me to care for my two daughters. A twelve-hour day at work can lead to an evening coma at home, so when Mom's punching little square buttons on a cash register, I hardly have the energy to pour corn flakes for my kids, let alone outline a research paper.

Going to college means making choices, some of which bring criticism. My neighbors, for example, hate my sickly, brown lawn sandwiched between their lush, green, spotless plots of earth, which would be the envy of any football field. Just walking to my mailbox can be an awful reminder of how pitiful my lawn looks when I receive an unforgiving scowl from one of the groundskeepers who live on either side of me. It is embarrassing to have such a colorless lawn, but it will have to wait because I want more out of life than a half-acre of green turf. Right now my time and money are tied up in college courses instead of fertilizer and weed killer.

But the toughest obstacle is having to take away time from those I love most. I am proud of the relationship I have with my wife and kids, so it tears my guts out when I have to look into my daughter's sad face and explain that I can't go to the Christmas program she's been practicing for weeks because I have a final exam. It's not easy to tell my three-year-old that I can't push her on the swings because I have a cause-and-effect paper to write, or tell my seven-year-old that I can't build a snowman because I have an argument essay to polish. As I tell my family that I can't go sledding with them, my wife lets out a big sigh, and my kids yell, "Pu-leeze, Daddy, can't you come with us?" At these times I wonder if my dream of a college education can withstand such an emotional battering, or if it is even worth it. But I keep on keeping on because I must set a good example for the four little eyes that are keeping watch over their daddy's every move. I must succeed and pass on to them the right attitude toward school. This time when I graduate, because of the hurdles I've overcome, there will be a celebration—a proper one.

THE POWER WITHIN
Preview
Year after year, teachers watch the latest group of college students arrive in their classrooms. After a while, an observant teacher can begin to predict, with pretty good accuracy, which students will succeed and which will not. As veteran teacher John Langan explains, the most important factor is not a student's IQ. Read on to discover the real secrets behind college (and life!) success.

THE POWER WITHIN

John Langan

In the first college writing class that I taught, I had a student who was drowning.

Gerald was a quiet young man who wore sunglasses, did not speak in class, and sat in the back of the room. I didn't know he was drowning until I collected a mid-semester assignment which asked students to write about what they had done—or not done—to take charge of their lives.

I still remember reading Gerald's essay, listening to the voice of a young person flooded with pain and regret. It was so moving I asked him if I could copy and share it with other students. He agreed, and then, several weeks later, he stopped coming to class and I never saw him again. All that remains are his words:

MY LIFE

Somewhere, a little piece of me is lost and crying. Someplace, deep in the shadows of my subconscious, a piece of my soul has sat down and anchored itself in defeat and is trying to pull me down into the darkness with it. This might sound strange to someone who is not familiar with the inner conflicts that can tear and pull at a person's soul until he begins to stop and sink in his own deep-hollow depths. But sinking doesn't take much. It takes only one little flaw which left unattended will grow and grow . . . until, like cancer, it consumes the soul.

I know now, and I have always known, that help comes first from within. I know that if one doesn't come to one's own rescue, then all is lost. I know it is time for me to look at myself, which I would rather avoid. But in order to break free of my own chains, I must look at myself.

I could relate the incidents of youth. I could tell of many past failures and what I think caused them. But I won't, for one example will show where I'm at. At the beginning of this summer, I set my goals. These goals consisted of the college courses I wanted to complete and where I wanted to be physically and mentally when the summer was over. Listed among the goals to be accomplished were courses I needed in writing and accounting. But now I am so far behind in both courses it looks as if I will fail them both. I ask myself, "Why?" I know that if I work enough, I can handle the courses. So why am I so lazy? Why is it that the things I seem to want most, I either give up or in some way do not strive for? These are the questions I must try to answer.

I think I've spent too much of my life just waiting for good things to come. I've waited for a magic rainbow to appear in the sky and to drop a pot of gold in my lap. I've been hurt so much in life, and I just wanted it handed to me.

But it's time for me to stop chasing rainbows. It's time to stop looking into the sky, waiting for help to arrive. It's time for me to start bailing the rot out of my mind, to stop dreaming and not acting, before I have nothing left to hope for. I can see now that I've never given it the total effort, that I've always been afraid I would fail or not measure up. So I've quit early. Instead of acting on my dreams, I've laid back and just drifted along. I've lived too much time in this world unfulfilled. I've got to make my dreams work. I must do this now, and what it takes is the doing. Somehow I must learn to succeed at success rather than at failure, and the time to start is now.

I have known other students over the years who, like Gerald, were involved in an inner battle. It's often clear they regard themselves as unlikely to succeed in school. They walk into the classroom carrying defeat on their shoulders the way other students carry textbooks under their arms.

I'd look at them slouching in their seats and staring into space and think, "What terrible things have gone on in their lives that they've quit already? They have so little faith in their ability to learn that they're not even trying." Such students often suddenly disappear one day, just as Gerald did, and no one pays much notice because they had already disappeared in spirit long before.

When I have seen such students with res-ignation in their eyes, I have wanted to shake them by the shoulders and say, "You are not dead. Be proud and pleased that you have brought yourself this far. Yes, life has probably been very hard, but you can still be someone. Get off the bench. Come onto the playing field. Give it a shot. You'll never learn to suc-ceed if you don't try."

Running from the Power Within

For years I have watched what happens when a school year unfolds. As the crunch of work begins, students are put up against the wall. Like it or not, they must define their role in school. There are only two roads to take. One road is to do the work: to click off the stereo or television, reject the invitation to go out, shut off the cell phone, stop everything and anything else, and go do the essentially lonely work that studying is. The other road is to escape the work.

Below I describe escape routes I've seen students take. If you see yourself in any of these situations, you need to recognize it. Self-knowledge is power. Once you are aware of what you are doing, you can begin to deal with it.

"I Can't Do It."

Some people let themselves be discouraged by bad grades. They think, "There's no use trying. I'm just not any good at this." But the only way people will really know that they cannot do something is by first trying—giving it their best shot. They must not let a defeatist attitude keep them from making a real effort. If you think you "can't do it," the reason may be that you have given up far too soon.

"I'm Too Busy."

Some people make themselves too busy, perhaps working more hours on a part-time job than they need to. Others get overly involved in social activities. Others allow personal or family problems to become so distracting that they cannot concentrate on their work. There are situations in which people are so busy or troubled that they cannot do their work. But there are also situations where people exaggerate conflicts or stress. They create an excuse for not doing what they know they should do.

"I'm Too Tired."

People with this excuse usually become tired as soon as it's time to write a paper or study a book or go to class. Their weariness clears up when the work period ends. The "sleepiness syndrome" also expresses itself in the imagined need for naps during the day and then ten hours or more of sleep at night. Such students are, often literally, closing their eyes to the hard work that school demands.

"I'll Do It Later."

Everyone tends at times to procrastinate—to put things off. Some students, however, constantly postpone assignments and study. Time and time again they put off what needs to be done so they can watch TV, talk to a friend, hang out with their peers, or do any one of a hundred other things. They typically wind up cramming for tests and writing last-minute papers, and they often seem surprised and angry at their low grades.

"I'm Bored with the Subject."

Students sometimes explain that they are doing poorly in a course because the instructor or the subject matter is boring. These students want education to be entertainment— an unrealistic expectation. On the whole, courses and instructors balance out: Some are boring, some are exciting, many are in between. If a course is not interesting, students should be all the more motivated to do the work so that they can leave the course behind once and for all.

"I'm Here, and That's What Counts."
Some students spend their time at school lost in a dangerous kind of fantasy. They feel, "All will be well, for here I am in school. I have a student ID in my pocket, a sweatshirt with the school name on it, and textbooks on my desk. All this proves I am a student." Such students have given in to a fantasy we all at times succumb to: the belief that we will get something for nothing. But we find out soon enough that such a hope is a false one. Life seldom gives us something for nothing—and school won't either.

We have probably all known students who escape. They make excuses. They never really determine to try their best. They know what they should do but don't do it. They fool themselves, time and time again. They try to have as much fun as they can, and they keep saying, "Tomorrow. Tomorrow I will get serious. Tomorrow I will start working hard." There is often a terrible hurt deep inside them. And for some reason a switch within never turns on, a spark of determination never ignites. They are individuals who are unable to take charge of their own lives and to work hard, as Gerald puts it, "to succeed at success."

Turning On the Power Within

Wouldn't it be great if we could go to a drug-store and buy motivational pills? These personal power pills would energize our attitude. We would turn on to success and take charge of our lives and pursue worthy goals. We would be determined and self-disciplined, and nothing would stop us. Of course, there are no such pills. What I am going to offer you instead are some thoughts. Read and think about them and see if you can get them into your soul.

Thought # 1:
Having a Dream

Several years ago, my wife and I were vacationing in New Mexico. As we drove into one small town, we suddenly came upon a huge billboard. I was so struck by what it said that I stopped our car and wrote down the words.

If you never have a dream, you'll never have a dream come *true*.

You need to have a dream within you—a belief and resolve in your heart that you will take charge of your life and make yourself proud.

Consider this basic truth about human nature: we all want to respect ourselves. We all want to live our lives in such a way that we think well of our behavior and others think well of us. We do not want to be disrespected or seen as bad people. An equally basic truth is that the only way we can get respect is to earn it. At a certain point in growing up, we realize that life doesn't give us something for nothing. What is important and meaningful is what we earn through trying hard and working hard.

Take a minute to think about the following question: Imagine two people. The first person has drifted unhappily through life, putting in a minimal effort at a series of jobs and maybe even at times living off others. One morning the telephone rings and someone says to this person, "Congratulations. You have just won a million dollars in the state lottery." The second person works hard and eventually earns a million dollars; that person is well-regarded by others and has a strong sense of accomplishment and self-worth. Which person would you rather be—the one who *won* a million dollars or the one who *earned* a million dollars?

Of course, we'd all like to wake up one morning and learn that we've just won a million dollars. But let's face it: this isn't very likely. In fact, it's close to impossible. So if you're realistic, chances are you would choose to be the person who worked hard, overcame obstacles, and achieved success. If you relate to that person, your attitude may be something like this: "I want to respect myself and have others respect me. To get this respect, I'm going to work hard to succeed. At this stage in my life, that means doing well in school because education is clearly a key to success." And if you've made mistakes in the past (and many of us have), your attitude should be: "I can change my behavior. I'm going to learn to work hard so I can get somewhere and be someone."

Thought #2
Your Attitude about Learning

Think about your own attitude toward learning. Put a check by the item or items that apply to you. (If you agree with some sentences in an item but not others, cross out the ones you do not agree with.)

_____ School has never really turned me on. I feel I can start to study if I need to, but I don't want to. What's wrong with being a bit lazy? Life is supposed to be about enjoying yourself and having some fun. I want to take it easy and have as much good time as I can for now.

_____ I suppose I am passive about studying, but it's not all my fault. I'm tired of being told what to do. I'm tired of being force-fed what other people think I need to learn. A lot of the stuff is not going to be of any value to me as far as I can see. I can't wait to get out of school and be on my own so I can start living my life.

_____ If I study too much, I'll miss out on the good times that school has to offer. I won't have time to go to games or parties. And I don't want to be alone. If I start studying, some of my friends are going to think twice about hanging out with me.

_____ I want to do more in school, but I'm afraid of really giving it a good effort. What if I try my best and I still get lousy grades? People will just laugh at me. I don't want to look foolish, so I'm probably just going to drift along and not call any attention to myself.

_____ I guess I've just been out of it for a long time. There are probably lots of reasons why. I never got any encouragement along the way. I pretty much just let things happen to me. I feel like a piece of driftwood that's been tossed about on a stormy sea. I do want to do something and to become someone. I've felt like this for a while, and at times I really want to get serious. But so far I just haven't done so.

_____ I'm not an active student who tries my best all the time. But I'm not a zombie either. I do some studying, just not as much as other people would like me to. I should probably do more, and I'm going to work on that and try to do a better job of taking charge of my studies.

_____ I feel something stirring within me. For a long time I was dead to learning, but now I want to get somewhere. I'm ready to be a serious student. It's true that some of the stuff I have to study is boring, and some teachers do not care. But I feel now that these are just hurdles that will not stop me. I'm going to start doing more to get where I want to go.

_____ I'm on the move, and I have taken charge of my life. There is something inside me that is strong and determined to succeed. I feel in my heart of hearts that nothing is going to stop me. It's my life, and I'm going to work hard and respect myself and gain success and happiness.

So where do you fit? The items above will help you think about what your attitude is and how you can improve it.

Thought #3
Doing the Work

The heart of the matter is not the speed at which a person learns; the heart of the matter is his or her determination—"I *will* learn." I have seen people who had this quality of determination or persistence do poorly in a course (often because of out-of-class problems or events), come back and repeat it, and finally succeed.

Through knowing such determined people, I've come to feel that the single most important factor for school survival and success is an inner commitment to doing the work. When the crunch comes—and the crunch is the plain hard work that school requires—the person with the commitment meets it head-on; the person without the commitment avoids it in a hundred different ways.

On the following scale of *Passive* to *Determined*, where would you rate yourself?

Passive 1 2 3 4 5 6 7 8 9 **10 Determined**

Why have you rated yourself at that point on the scale? What strengths can you build upon? What are the personal challenges you must overcome?

Thought # 4
An Unequal Playing Field

There is a popular idea in America that has always made me uneasy. It is the idea that success is within us—that we can all "pull ourselves up by our bootstraps" and triumph over tough odds.

Now there is truth to this idea, but it is not the whole truth. Life is like a race, and there are different lanes on the racetrack. Some of us are in lanes where there are no obstacles on the track. Some of us are in lanes where there are all kinds of obstacles—for example, personal health challenges, family neglect or abuse, poverty, racism, a neighborhood environment with violence and drugs, a school where one's peers are not into studies but into "respecting themselves" by being in the right clique, wearing the right kind of footwear, having the right hair style, or whatever.

If you're on a track that is full of obstacles, you can get worn down. You can start losing hope. And then it is harder to ignite the spark of determination within. In such circumstances, you must try your best to be a hero. You must battle the odds. You must keep alive a belief deep inside yourself that you can make your world a better one. And the first step in doing that is to realize your life has been hard, but you will not give up. If you have read this essay so far, chances are that you can do it. You can be a fighter. You can be a hero.

Thought # 5
A Quotation to Live By

If I could pass along one quotation, it would be this line from the great religious and political leader Mahatma Gandhi: **"Be the change you want to see in the world."** These ten words are all simple ones, but put together they express an idea with unlimited power. The key to changing your world is to take personal responsibility for your action and behavior. No one else can do this for you; it must be you alone.

To put Gandhi's idea another way, each one of us has his or her own ship to sail. Some people don't sail their own ships; they just kind of drift with the tides. That's not a very satisfying way to live one's life, just drifting along with others who are also drifting, and yet a lot of people do it. If their friends and peers are into enjoying the moment and taking the easy way out and not into setting larger goals in life, that's what they do.

I urge you to actively sail your own ship. That ship of yours is unique and precious, and no one else should sail it for you. That ship is the journey of your life. You get to go on that journey only once, and it's a one-way ticket, so make the most of it. Dream dreams, set meaningful goals, make something happen. Don't just drift along with the tides. Become someone.

In the opening story, my student Gerald realized he was not sailing his own ship, and you could almost hear him crying out in disillusionment and regret. Do not let that happen to you. You do not want to wake up some day with a taste of ashes and dust in your mouth and a terrible pain in your soul.

Thought # 6
The Fear of Loneliness

Perhaps the biggest reason it is so hard to take responsibility for one's life and sail one's own ship is the fear of being alone.

To grow, we must sometimes set sail in new directions and leave acquaintances and friends behind. At such times, we must have the courage and strength to depend on ourselves. We must be ready to handle the loneliness that may be part of marching to the beat of our own drummer. We must not cling to the crowd when it prevents our personal growth. When the adventurer Columbus set sail for America, it was a terrifying thing to do. But he discovered a new world, and if we have the courage to sail our own ship, so might we.

Thought #7
The Opportunity to Help Others

There are many self-help books on the market that present the following idea: If you take charge of your life, you can achieve financial success. That may (or may not) be true, but it is not the full story of what happiness is about. As you seek to grow, the larger goal to keep in mind is that by gaining power for yourself, you will gain the power to be of help to others.

Robert Kennedy said, "The purpose of life is to contribute in some way to making things better." Dr. Martin Luther King wrote, "Life's most persistent and urgent question is, 'What are you doing for others?'" If we take control of our lives and achieve a measure of success, we will have the opportunity to work on behalf of others. At that stage, many religious leaders believe, we become fully blessed.

Thought #8
The Power of Regular Reading

If you have read this essay so far, you may be saying, "OK, I'm ready to do what it takes. I'll stick to my studies because I know they're a means to an end. I'll have some fun and games but remember they're a side show and not the main event. I'm OK with being alone a bit along the way. But what else can I do to keep myself inspired? What practical strategy do you have for me?"

I do have one strategy: Read. No one expresses better than Oprah Winfrey the power of reading: "I can't imagine," she said, "how I could have become the person I am now without books. How would I know there was another world beyond my small, isolated, feeling-abandoned world? Books became synonymous with freedom. They showed that you can open doors and walk through."

Many people (and I am one of them) believe that regular reading is the very heart of education. Here is what the experts say:

1. Reading provides language power. Research has shown *beyond any question* that frequent reading improves vocabulary, spelling, and reading speed and comprehension, as well as grammar and writing style. If you become a regular reader, all of these language and thinking abilities develop almost automatically.

2. Reading increases the chances for job success. In today's world more than ever before, jobs involve the processing of information, with words being the tools of the trade. Studies have found that the better your command of words, the more success you are likely to have. Nothing will give you a command of words like regular reading.

3. Reading creates human power. Reading enlarges the mind and the heart. It frees us from the narrow confines of our own experience. Knowing how other people view important matters helps us decide what we ourselves think and feel. Reading also helps us connect with others and realize our shared humanity. The novelist C.S. Lewis wrote, "We read in order to know that we are not alone." We become less isolated as we share the common experiences, emotions, and thoughts that make us human. We grow more sympathetic and understanding because we realize that others are like us.

Regular reading can, in short, change your life. It can open the door to a lifetime of pleasure, learning, and personal growth. But you must be the one to decide whether to walk through that door.

If you want a list of some good books to help you get started reading, see the back of this book.

Finally . . .

There are no fireworks to set off here, just some final words.

Understand that your ship is yours alone to sail, and no one else can sail it for you. The power within you is enormous, but you must turn it on. Work on your studies. Reread this essay. Order some books. I wish you a strong and courageous heart as you set sail on the adventure of your life.

AFTERWORD

Consider these two wise sayings:

"If you keep doing the things you've always done, you'll get the same results you've always had."

"Insanity is doing the same thing over and over again, but expecting different results."

Do you see the common theme? Here's another way of putting it: If you are not satisfied with the way your life is going, maybe it's time to look inside. Are you doing the same ineffective things over and over, yet expecting different results? Are you waiting for your circumstances to change, or the people around you to change, or your job or your spouse or your teachers or your income or your mood to change? Do you spend lots of time thinking, "If only _____ would happen, THEN I'd be able to make real changes in my life?" If so, this book is for you.

It's human nature to think, "Things will get better, and *then* I'll succeed." But the fact is that this is rarely the case. Successful people succeed because they have learned the habits of success. Instead of waiting for circumstances to change, they change their circumstances. Instead of waiting around for a better future, they create their own futures—a step at a time, but steadily.

Maybe that sounds like an awful lot of work. Maybe you think, "Yeah, but my circumstances are different. Until my situation changes, there's not much I can do." Maybe the idea of changing your own life sounds overwhelming.

But the reality is that *you* hold the power to be successful. Not fate, not luck, not other people, not events over which you have no control—*you*.

Just for now, try to turn off the voice in your head that says, "Yeah, but *I* can't do that. *My* situation is different. It's complicated."

That voice is the voice of defeat. Don't listen to it. You CAN "do that." You DON'T have to wait to win the lottery. You DON'T have to wait until your friends or your parents or your spouse says, "OK, go ahead and change your life." You DON'T have to wait until you are feeling ambitious and energetic. You can decide, right this minute, "No matter what anybody else says or does, I am going to start living as a motivated, successful person." You can begin breaking old, self-defeating habits and adding new, positive habits to your life—today. Making that decision and getting started will be, by far, the most difficult part of the process. With every minute, day, and hour you practice your new habits, the easier they will get. You will begin seeing positive improvements in your life. You will feel proud and happy about your progress. Success will breed success.

Consider the examples—positive and negative—of some of the people you've met in this book:

Let's start with the young army wife described by Scott Peck in his essay "Responsibility." She is with her husband, stationed in Japan. She's homesick and miserable.

So far, it's easy to sympathize with the young woman. It's hard to be far away from family and friends and living in a foreign culture, unable to speak the local language.

But Dr. Peck offers a simple way that the young woman could improve her situation. She could drive her husband to work, then spend time in the American housing area where she might make friends. That's impossible, the woman tells him. The car is a stick shift, and she can't drive a stick shift. Furthermore, she tells Peck angrily, she has no intention of learning to drive a stick shift.

So she is left miserable, self-pitying, and lonely, refusing to take action that would help herself. She would rather think of herself as a victim, demanding that other people change for her, than become an active participant in her own life.

Not a very flattering picture, is it?

The reader can hope that the young woman eventually reached a turning point in her life, something like the one that Peggy Kern describes in her essay "Raising the Blinds." Like the young army wife, Peggy had handed the reins of her life over to someone else—in this case, her college boyfriend. Sinking back into a childlike state, Peggy allowed her boyfriend to make all the decisions for her as well as him. Even as she saw the toll that her inaction was taking, she remained passive, letting the situation slip further and further out of her control. It took a serious shock to waken Peggy to the fact that she, not her boyfriend or anyone else, was responsible for her life and decisions. At that point, she found the motivation to succeed.

Paul Logan, the author of "Zero," reached a similar turning point. Like Peggy, he essentially threw away his first college semester. Depressed and discouraged, he dropped out and took a job doing manual labor. His humiliation reached a peak when he ran into a group of former high school friends, home from college on their spring break.

At that point, it would have been easy for Paul, like the young army wife, to sink even deeper into self-pity and depression. He could have blamed his college teachers for allowing him to fail. He could have blamed his college friends for being available when he wanted to party. He could have bitterly decided he wasn't "college material" and settled for a lifetime of unfulfilling jobs. But he didn't do any of those things. He saved his money and courageously returned to college—this time with an attitude that did not allow room for failure.

Then there's Dawn Cogliser. Of the people in this book, Dawn perhaps more than anyone else could have justified sinking into a state of depression and inaction. Abused by her parents, her stepfather, her stepgrandfather, and her husband; homeless and substance-dependent; Dawn could easily have said, "It's hopeless; there's nothing I can do" and allowed her life to simply slip away. Instead, she found the incredible courage to turn her back on her former existence and pursue a new way of life.

Not all the contributors to the book tell their own personal stories. Some, like educator John Langan and surgeon Ben Carson, give us the benefit of their observations of students who make it and those who do not. Their stories make it clear that whatever their circumstances, people who are focused and motivated have an enormous head start over those who are merely drifting along.

Enjoy the stories in this book. May you find hope and inspiration in them. If they sometimes make you feel uncomfortable—if you see your past behavior reflected in them in unflattering ways—use that discomfort as a motivating force. Use it as Dawn Cogliser uses the memory of the taste in her mouth after her near-fatal beating: "I have never let myself forget the taste of that blood and those tears. The memory motivates me to keep moving forward towards all the great things that life has to offer me."

This afterward began with two wise sayings. It ends with an excerpt from a poem by Amado Nervo, a Mexican poet. The poem is called "At Peace." In his old age, the poet is looking back at his life, and he says:

> I saw at the end of my life's journey that I was the architect of my own destiny.
>
> If I extracted the sweetness or the bitterness of things, it was because I put the sweetness or the bitterness in them.
>
> When I planted rose bushes, I always harvested roses.

Let these beautiful words remind you: You, and only you, are the architect of your own destiny. May you find the courage to make the most of your life's journey.

SOME GOOD BOOKS TO READ

All of the following books are available for $1 each from Townsend Press at **www. townsend press.com**. If you have never been much of a reader, we'd suggest that you start with one of the books in the first column.

Reading Changed My Life!
Letters My Mother
   Never Read
Ten Real-Life Stories
Surviving Abuse
Facing Addiction
It Couldn't Happen to Me
Everyday Heroes
Lost and Found
A Matter of Trust
Secrets in the Shadows
Someone to Love Me
The Bully
The Gun
Until We Meet Again
Blood Is Thicker
Brothers in Arms
Summer of Secrets
The Fallen
Shattered
Search for Safety
Great Stories of Suspense
   and Adventure
Narrative of the Life of
   Frederick Douglass
Jane Eyre
The Story of Blima
Dracula
The Jungle Book
The Mark of Zorro
Ragged Dick
Tarzan of the Apes
Black Beauty
Up from Slavery
Incidents in the Life of a
   Slave Girl
Captains Courageous

Uncle Tom's Cabin
Laughter and Chills
The War of the Worlds
White Fang
The Call of the Wild
The Return of Tarzan
The Beasts of Tarzan
Treasure Island
The Wind in the Willows
The Wizard of Oz
A Princess of Mars
The Gods of Mars
The Warlord of Mars
Robin Hood
Tom Sawyer
Huckleberry Finn
The Prince and the Pauper
Frankenstein/Dr. Jekyll and
   Mr. Hyde
The Hound of the Baskervilles
Robinson Crusoe
The Scarlet Letter
Ethan Frome
The Red Badge of Courage
The Virginian
Swiss Family Robinson
King Arthur and His Knights
The Return of the Native
Pride and Prejudice
Silas Marner
Sister Carrie
Gulliver's Travels
Great Expectations
A Tale of Two Cities
The Last of the Mohicans
The Odyssey
Foster Care Odyssey

SOME TOWNSEND LIBRARY BOOKS

Titles and descriptions of some Townsend Library books appear on the following pages.

Reading Changed My Life!
Three True Stories

After a lifetime of abuse, Maria Cardenas was finally living in peace with her daughter. But soon, that little girl would be able to read better than her mother. What could Maria do?

School was a nightmare for Daisy Russell. She couldn't wait to get away from a place where she felt stupid and worthless. But once she dropped out, she discovered a burning desire to learn to read. Was it too late?

As a child, Julia Burney escaped from the poverty and violence of her home into a world of books. As an adult, she saw children growing up without that escape available to them. How could she help?

In *Reading Changed My Life! Three True Stories*, you'll learn what happened to Maria, Daisy, and Julia. They are three courageous women whose stories will touch and inspire you.

Letters My Mother Never Read

When her mother died in a fire, eight-year-old Jerri thought life couldn't get worse. She was wrong. Sent to live with people who didn't want her, Jerri was powerless to stop her once-happy childhood from becoming a nightmare of cruelty and neglect. Only a stubborn belief in her own worth and a fierce will to live allowed her to reach adulthood physically and emotionally intact. This is a book that will inspire not only those who have been orphans or foster children, but anyone who has known the pain of being unwanted.

Everyday Heroes

Everyday Heroes tells the moving stories of twenty real-life men and women who have faced—and overcome—serious challenges in their lives. The people in the book are not the media-created "heroes" of our sports or entertainment worlds. They are ordinary people who can be seen as heroes because they have had the courage to stand up to life's difficulties. The multicultural stories and accompanying photographs (there are three photos of each subject) will inspire readers to take charge of their lives and to do their best.

Surviving Abuse

"Abuse" is an ugly word. And to many people, abuse is an ugly reality of life. This book tells the true stories of two men and two women whose lives have been painfully marked by abuse.

As a child, Kenyon was beaten first by his mother, later by his father and stepmother.

Dawn grew up surrounded by abusive people, then married a violent man.

Ryan's stepfather terrorized his entire family, physically and emotionally.

Eunice was only a child when an adult relative targeted her for sexual abuse.

The things that Kenyon, Dawn, Ryan, and Eunice experienced could have destroyed them inside. But that's not what happened. Read *Surviving Abuse* to learn how people can grow strong and healthy even after suffering at the hands of others.

Facing Addiction

It's easy to quit using drugs and alcohol. Just ask Gwen, Miguel, and John. They've done it dozen of times.

The hard part is not starting again.

These true stories describe three people's descent into addiction and their struggles to recover.

Gritty and sad, painful and inspiring, these stories show both how low the human spirit can fall and how, against all odds, it can rise again.

Great Stories of Suspense and Adventure

In this book, six spine-tingling experiences await you:

In *Rikki-Tikki-Tavi,* you'll visit a sun-baked garden in India, where silent death lurks in the tall grass.

In *The Monkey's Paw,* you'll be given a gift of three wishes you'll wish you hadn't received.

In *Leiningen Versus the Ants,* on a lush plantation in Brazil, you'll battle an army of tiny soldiers who turn a man into a skeleton in the blink of an eye.

In *The Lady, or the Tiger?* you'll be on trial for your life, and your fate will rest in the hands of a friend who just might wish you dead.

In *To Build a Fire,* deep in the frozen Yukon north, you'll confront a danger that's beyond human understanding.

In *The Most Dangerous Game,* on a tropical island, you'll meet a charming fellow who loves to hunt—and who has chosen you as his target.

It Couldn't Happen to Me
Three True Stories of Teenage Moms

Johanna, Rasheedah, and Rachel: each became an unmarried mother while she was still in her teens. With the birth of her baby, each girl's "ordinary" teen life was over.

Johanna's boyfriend acted happy when he heard she was pregnant. But as her pregnancy progressed, she saw less and less of him. Soon after the baby's birth, he went to jail. How would she support a baby without even a high school diploma?

After Rasheedah's baby was born, all she could do was cry. She didn't know anything about babies. She didn't even dare touch this screaming, demanding stranger. Her depression grew as her dreams of college vanished into thin air.

Rachel wanted to be popular. Boys liked her. But she also wanted to save her reputation. When she discovered she was pregnant, she told a lie—one that would haunt her until her daughter was born.

Johanna, Rasheedah, and Rachel are three of today's teen moms. They have offered to share their stories so that other young girls won't make the mistake of thinking, "It couldn't happen to me."

Ten Real-Life Stories

As you read *Ten Real-Life Stories*, you will meet a fascinating variety of people. The one thing they have in common is that they are real. So are their stories.

Here are a few of the people you will learn about:

- Vingo, a man released from prison, going home to a wife who may not want him.
- Richard, a little boy who "invented" a father to hide his embarrassment.
- Paul, so afraid of bullying that he betrayed a friend at school.
- Lupe, a "retarded" girl who wasn't.
- Ben, whose mother would not allow him to fail.
- Marvel, who fooled everyone into believing she could read.
- Jean, who found that education could counter the hard blows of life.

Up from Slavery: An Autobiography

Born into slavery, Booker T. Washington is freed when he is nine years old.

To help support his family, he then works as a salt packer, coal miner, and house servant. All the while, he longs to become educated and to educate others. Poverty, racism, and other obstacles stand in his way. Will he overcome them all, or will the many barriers prove stronger than his unwavering determination?

Narrative of the Life of Frederick Douglass

Frederick Douglass was born a slave, denied an education, and expected to work like a beast of the fields until the day he died. But Douglass's mind and spirit could not be imprisoned. As he secretly learned to read and write, Douglass looked ahead to the day he could escape the chains of slavery. Once free, he wrote this classic of American literature. It is a story that shocked the world with its first-hand account of the horrors of slavery.

The Story of Blima: A Holocaust Survivor

In 1941, Blima Weisstuch was a young Jewish woman going about her life in a city in Poland.

She paid no heed to the stories about a man named Adolf Hitler, his Nazi Party, and their plan for a world that did not include Jews.

But almost overnight her ordinary life was gone, replaced by a nightmare world of terror and death. Millions of people disappeared into the horror of the Holocaust. But Blima's story survives. It is told here by her daughter, Shirley Russak Wachtel.

Incidents in the Life of a Slave Girl

Born into slavery, Harriet Jacobs has no rights— not even the right to marry the man she loves.

Instead, she is faced with the demands of a master who believes he is entitled not only to her labor, but also to her body. Only great courage, wit, and determination will allow Harriet to preserve her self-respect—and someday win her freedom. This autobiography tells the true story of a remarkable woman.

The Jungle Book

Born a man; raised by wolves. Where does Mowgli belong? A human baby is saved from the jaws of a hungry tiger. Mother and Father Wolf accept it as their own; the angry tiger, Shere Khan, swears he will have his revenge. As little Mowgli grows up in the jungle of India, he feels safe and happy with his wolf brothers and sisters, Bagheera the black panther, and Baloo the bear. But his friends know the awful truth: the day will come when Mowgli will have to confront Shere Khan alone.

Dracula

Jonathan Harker has a job to do. The young lawyer must go to the mysterious country of Transylvania to work for a man he knows as "the Count." At first, Jonathan is excited by the chance to travel and meet new people. But after his arrival in Transylvania, he begins to wonder what's going on. People act strangely upon hearing he is going to visit the Count. When Jonathan arrives at the Count's dark, isolated castle, he too begins to feel afraid. Soon after meeting his host, Jonathan finds himself trapped in a horrifying nightmare. Only this nightmare is real, and he can't wake up. . . .

Tarzan of the Apes

Without his animal strength and human intelligence, Tarzan of the Apes would many times have been a dead man. Orphaned in infancy, Tarzan is adopted by a female ape who has just lost her own baby. Against all odds, he survives and learns the ways of the great apes. But Tarzan is different from the apes, and he knows this more with each passing day. Then he comes face-to-face with a beautiful woman named Jane, and, more than ever, he wonders just who the real Tarzan is.

Jane Eyre

A poor, unwanted orphan, Jane Eyre seems destined to live a sad and ordinary life.

But chance has brought her to Thornfield, home of Mr. Rochester, and secrets no one will explain. Who is the laughing woman in the third-floor room? What dark memories torment Mr. Rochester? Can a governess help the master of Thornfield Hall overcome the horror of his past? Or will that past haunt them both . . . forever?

Ragged Dick

Fourteen-year-old Dick Hunter lives on the streets of New York in the 1860s.

His parents are dead, and he has been on his own since the age of seven. He shines shoes to earn a living. He sleeps in boxes. He jokes about having a mansion on Fifth Avenue and about owning shares of Erie Railroad stock. But he cannot imagine ever being more than a boot-black who spends every cent he earns and lives hand-to-mouth—until by chance he meets Frank Whitney.

SOME BOOKS FROM THE BLUFORD SERIES

Lost and Found

Darcy Wills has major problems. And she does not know where to turn for help. First there was the mysterious stranger who started following her. Then there was the threatening note left on her desk at Bluford High School. And now her sister has disappeared. Forced into a desperate race against time, Darcy must take action to save her sister—and her fragile family—before it is too late.

Someone To Love Me

At first, Bobby Wallace was everything Cindy Gibson hoped for. He was friendly, seemingly mature, and handsome—the perfect escape from her problems in school and even bigger troubles at home. But then, Bobby starts behaving strangely, and Cindy gets scared. Hiding her concerns from her friends and her distracted mother, Cindy soon finds herself in the worst trouble of her life.

The Bully

A new life. A new school. A new bully. That's what Darrell Mercer faces when he and his mother move from Philadelphia to California. After spending months living in fear, Darrell is faced with a big decision. He can either keep on running from this bully—or find some way to fight back.

The Gun

Tyray Hobbs wants revenge. Weeks ago he was one of the most feared students in Bluford High. But then Darrell Mercer publicly humiliated him, and Tyray lost his reputation. To get it back, he must take down Darrell. But how?

With a broken hand, a troubled family, and no friends in sight, Tyray's options are limited. And when the kids he once bullied start threatening him, his world completely unravels. Desperate to settle the score and regain respect, Tyray sees only one solution to his problems—a gun.

Search for Safety

There is no escape for Ben McKee. For weeks, he's covered the bruises on his body. He's even lied to his teachers and new friends at Bluford High School. But the trouble in Ben's house isn't going away. And if he doesn't act soon, it could swallow him and his mother forever.

Brothers in Arms

Martin Luna is in deep trouble. And there is no easy way out.

Just months ago, a horrible tragedy took his little brother, and now it threatens to take him, too. On one side are his desperate mother, a friendly teacher at Bluford High School, and a pretty girl named Vicky. On the other are his homeboys, his old neighborhood, and his hunger for revenge. Torn between the two, Martin stands at a crossroad, with his life hanging in the balance. Which way will he go?

To encourage reading, Townsend Press offers many paperback books at the special price of $1 a book. See all the books in the Townsend Library—and even read the first chapter in each one—at

www.townsendpress.com